FORERUNNERS: IDEAS FIRST
FROM THE UNIVERSITY OF MINNESOTA PRESS

Original e-works to spark new scholarship

FORERUNNERS: IDEAS FIRST is a thought-in-process series of breakthrough digital publications. Written between fresh ideas and finished books, Forerunners draws on scholarly work initiated in notable blogs, social media, conference plenaries, journal articles, and the synergy of academic exchange. This is gray literature publishing: where intense thinking, change, and speculation take place in scholarship.

D1316908

DEEP MAPPING THE
MEDIA CITY

Deep Mapping the Media City

SHANNON MATTERN

University of Minnesota Press

Minneapolis

Portions of this book were published in a different form in "Ear to the Wire: Listening to Historic Urban Infrastructures," *Amodern* 2 (Fall 2013), http://amodern.net/article/ear-to-the-wire/, and in "Deep Time of Media Infrastructure," in *Signal Traffic: Critical Studies of Media Infrastructures,* edited by Lisa Parks and Nicole Starosielski (Champaign, Ill.: University of Illinois Press, forthcoming).

Published by the University of Minnesota Press, 2015
111 Third Avenue South, Suite 290
Minneapolis, MN 55401-2520
http://www.upress.umn.edu

The University of Minnesota is an equal-opportunity educator and employer.

Contents

Preface

If IBM had ever bothered to actually possess a physical country, that country might have had a lot in common with Singapore. . . . We can all be suitably impressed with Singapore's evident willingness to view such technology with the utmost seriousness. In terms of applied tech, they seem to have an awfully practical handle on what this stuff can do. The National Computer Board has designed an immigration system capable of checking foreign passports in 30 seconds, resident passports in fifteen. Singapore's streets are planted with sensor loops to register real-time traffic; the traffic lights are computer controlled, and the system adjusts itself constantly to optimize the situation, creating "green waves" whenever possible. A different sort of green wave will appear if a building's fire sensor calls for help; emergency vehicles are automatically green-lighted through to the source of the alarm. The physical operation of the city's port, constant and quite unthinkably complex, is managed by another system. A "smart-card" system is planned to manage billings for cars entering the Restricted Zone . . .

They're good at this stuff. Really good. But now they propose to become something else as well; a coherent city of information, its architecture planned from the ground up. And they expect that whole highways of data will flow into and through their city.

—WILLIAM GIBSON, "Disneyland with the Death Penalty,"
Wired

THUS WROTE WILLIAM GIBSON in *Wired* magazine's fourth issue, way back in 1993. That's about twenty years before all of the "ubiquitous computing" hullaballoo of today—before cities like Rio, Incheon, and Helsinki joined up with the likes of IBM and Cisco to make their supposedly dumb cities smart.[1] This urban "enlightenment" includes open-data initiatives and urban informatics projects to aid in wayfinding, traffic flow, service discovery, even the location of hazardous cracks in the sidewalk.

Widespread academic, professional, and popular concern with infrastructures, particularly with the material networks that make our seemingly immaterial systems work, or work better, seems to be part of the zeitgeist. In addition to the corporately managed projects, we also have citizen-led walking tours of cell phone antenna networks, crowd-sourced maps of bike routes and sewage systems, blue-chip gallery exhibitions featuring photos of data centers and e-waste deposits, interactive maps of transoceanic fiber-optic cables, and hacking and circuit-bending workshops where kids explore the guts of their iPhones. Jussi Parikka regards many of these artistic and design practices as methods for both creatively and critically exploring "subaltern discourses, local knowledges, . . . [and] the material basis of communication technologies"—particularly the "singularity of . . . material assemblages."[2] These are among the central concerns of

1. See http://smartercitieschallenge.org/city_helsinki_finland.html; http://www.forumvirium.fi/en/project-areas/smart-city.

2. Jussi Parikka and Garnet Hertz, "Archaeologies of Media Art," *CTheory* (April 2010), http://www.ctheory.net/articles.aspx?id=631.

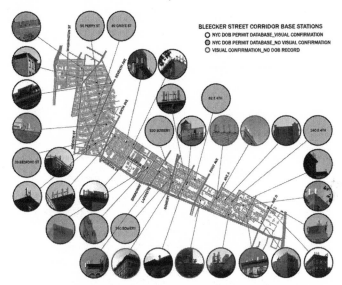

Figure 1. Walking Tour of Cell-Phone Infrastructure. Courtesy Michael Chen and Justin Snider, Michael Chen Architecture. Imagery copyright 2014, Aerodata International Surveys, Cnes/Spot Image, DigitalGlobe, GeoContent, Landsat. Map data copyright 2014, Google.

media archaeology, which offers a theoretical framework and set of methods that can help us trace the "smart" genome in our cities all the way back to Rome—and even, I argue, to Uruk and Çatalhöyük.

Yet when we're looking at urban communication networks, which are my primary concern, we're never looking solely at media. We're looking at media networks that are plugged into and dependent on myriad other infrastructural networks: our telecommunications networks need electricity, the Internet needs plenty of chilled water to cool the servers and roads to deploy its fiber-optic cable layers and service technicians, and all depend to some degree on biopower.[3] Particularly in cities, Friedrich Kittler reminds us, "networks overlap upon other networks."[4] Plus, in seeking to learn more about how our urban media work—or don't work—there's only so much we can discern from disassembling our cell phones, radios, and routers. As the editors of a special "network archaeology" issue of the journal *Amodern* suggest, we might need to "unfocus" our attention on "media artifacts and their representations" and, instead, follow the wires and waves that extend out from those devices to explore the spaces of various scales in which nodes in the network connect.[5]

As we head into a future offering ever more potential for mediated control of the urban landscape and, at the same time, a pervasive sense of our loss of control over the proliferation and often uncritical application of technologies, we would do well to enlighten ourselves (rather than merely our cities) about what kind of "smartness" or "sentience" we want our cities to embody—and to encourage in its inhabitants. And doing so, I argue, requires that we also recognize that today's smart cities don't have a monopoly on urban

3. Much of the material on the next few pages is drawn from my "Ear to the Wire: Listening to Historic Urban Infrastructures," *Amodern* 2 (Fall 2013), http://amodern.net/article/ear-to-the-wire/.

4. Friedrich A. Kittler, "The City Is a Medium," *New Literary History* 27, no. 4 (1996): 719.

5. Nicole Starosielski, Braxton Soderman, and Chris Cheek, "Introduction: Network Archaeology," *Amodern* 2 (Fall 2013), http://amodern.net/article/network-archaeology/.

Figure 2. Antennae. Jens Schott Knudsen, http://www.pamhule.com/.

intelligence. Cities have embodied networked smarts and forms of "ambient" intelligence since long before the digital and what we know today as "the network."[6] Our cities have been mediated, and intelligent, for millennia.

What tools might we use to examine the material assemblages that have long made our cities "smart"? Or, to use a now-hackneyed phrase, how might we "make visible the invisible" infrastructures that power urban life? What if we took media and network archaeology literally, and borrowed a few tricks from archaeologists of the Indiana Jones, rather than Friedrich Kittler, variety? What if we picked up their

6. Malcolm McCullough's *Ambient Commons: Attention in the Age of Embodied Information* (Cambridge, Mass.: MIT Press, 2003) provides a very helpful genealogy of the term *ambient*.

Figure 3. Tangled Overhead Wires, New Delhi, by Steve. https://www
.flickr.com/photos/sasqrd/10669298/, CC BY-NC2.0.

towels and surveying tools? In the introduction to their 2011
anthology, Jussi Parikka and Erkki Huhtamo propose that
"media archaeology should not be confused with archaeology as a discipline. When media archaeologists claim that
they are 'excavating' media-cultural phenomena, the word
should be understood in a specific way."[7] Yet there's much
to be gained in a study of media-networked sites, like any
city, by considering how archaeologists proper understand

7. Erkki Huhtamo and Jussi Parikka, "Introduction: An Archae-
ology of Media Archaeology," in *Media Archaeology: Approaches,
Applications, and Implications*, ed. Eriki Huhtamo and Jussi Parikka
(Los Angeles: University of California Press, 2011), 3.

excavation—how they dig both metaphorically and literally into physical terrain—and by productively "confusing" media archaeology and archaeology proper.[8]

I'm advocating for an "urban media archaeology," a materialist, multisensory approach to exploring the deep material history—that is, a cultural materialist history that acknowledges the physicality, the "stuff" of history and culture—of our media cities. This approach has taken shape through my various research projects and classes over the past decade or so and, since 2010, has been put into action as a methodology in one of my graduate studios at the New School.[9] I certainly don't intend to exacerbate the proliferation of "archaeologies" we've witnessed in recent years—the past decade has brought books offering archaeologies of materiality,

8. John Durham Peters elucidates the value of considering parallels between media studies and *geology*, whose methodologies bear some resemblance to archaeology proper. The methodological concerns he addresses—for example, that geological "texts cannot be interpreted apart from an interpretation of the processes that produced them," that geologists "study not only content [of those texts], but signal and channel properties as well," that geologists face the "problem of belated reception, interpreting messages that come posthumously," that geologists must "draw inferences from an incomplete record of deep time"—are concerns that shovel-wielding media archaeologists must face as well. Peters, "Space, Time and Communication Theory," *Canadian Journal of Communication* 28, no. 4 (2003), http://www.cjc-online.ca/index.php/journal/article/view/1389/1467.

9. See my Urban Media Archaeology and Media and Architecture courses: http://www.wordsinspace.net/wordpress/teaching/course-list/urban-media-archaeology/ and http://www.wordsinspace.net/wordpress/teaching/course-list/media-and-architecture/.

memory, colonialism, vision, trade, conflict, attachment, and the future, among other sites and concepts—but I do want to differentiate my approach from existing media archaeological approaches, most of which regard "archaeology" metaphorically or as a Foucauldian methodology and exclude insights from archaeologists of the trowel-wielding variety. Unlike these prevailing approaches, I aim to examine—through sight, sound, touch, and so on—the material spaces in which our networks entangle themselves.[10] I'm investigating our material urban spaces as infrastructures for mediation, and I'm proposing that archaeological tools, like excavation and mapping, might help us to acknowledge and understand our smart, mediated cities in the longue durée.

10. Bjørnar Olsen, Michael Shanks, Timothy Webmoor, and Christopher Witmore, "Archaeology: The Discipline of Things," prospectus, Stanford Humanities Lab, http://humanitieslab.stanford.edu/23/1572?view=print; see also Bjørnar Olsen, Michael Shanks, Timothy Webmoor, and Christopher Witmore, *Archaeology: The Discipline of Things* (Berkeley: University of California Press, 2012).

The Deep Time of Urban Mediation

MUCH MEDIA ARCHAEOLOGICAL WORK challenges the "newness" of new media, demonstrating, as Lisa Gitelman does, that media are "always already new" and that, at one time or another, all "old technologies were new," as Carolyn Marvin reminds us. Likewise, we must question the newness—or rather the *modernity*—of the media city.

There's a plethora of research on architecture and cities in relation to mechanically reproduced still and moving images.[1] For instance, many photographic, architectural, and cultural historians, inspired greatly by Walter Benjamin, have examined the city as a photographic subject; photography's early role in the documentation of urban transformation and as an instigator of social change; and photography's influence on particular modern architectural and

1. Much of the material in this literature review section also appears in my "Deep Time of Media Infrastructure," in *Signal Traffic: Critical Studies of Media Infrastructures*, ed. Lisa Parks and Nicole Starosielski (Champaign: University of Illinois Press, forthcoming).

urban designers.[2] There's also a tremendous amount of work on the city and film as contemporaneous developments; on the representation of the city *in* film (this has historically been the dominant thread of investigation); on film production in the city; and on film's influence on architects and planners, and vice versa.[3] There's great interest in other

2. James Ackerman, *Origins, Imitations, Conventions: Representation in the Visual Arts* (Cambridge, Mass.: MIT Press, 2002); Beatriz Colomina, *Privacy and Publicity: Architecture as Mass Media* (Cambridge, Mass.: MIT Press, 1994); Peter Bacon Hales, *Silver Cities: Photographing American Urbanization, 1839–1915* (Philadelphia: Temple University Press, 1983); Neil Levine, "'The Significance of Facts': Mies's Collages Up Close and Personal," *Assemblage* 37 (December 1998): 70–101; Richard Pare, *Photography and Architecture: 1839–1939* (Montreal: Canadian Center for Architecture, 1982); Shelley Rice, *Parisian Views* (Cambridge, Mass.: MIT Press, 1999).

3. Walter Benjamin, *Illuminations*, trans. Harry Zohn (New York: Schocken Books, 1969); David B. Clarke, ed., *The Cinematic City* (New York: Routledge, 1997); Colomina, *Privacy and Publicity*, 1994; Edward Dimendberg, *Film Noir and the Spaces of Modernity* (Cambridge, Mass.: Harvard University Press, 2004); Sergei Eisenstein, "Montage and Architecture," trans. Michael Glenny, *Assemblage* 10 (1938/1989): 111–31; Richard Koszarski, *Hollywood on the Hudson: Film and Television in New York from Griffith to Sarnoff* (New Brunswick, N.J.: Rutgers University Press, 2010); Ranjani Mazumdar, *Bombay Cinema: An Archive of the City* (Minneapolis: University of Minnesota Press, 2007); Scott McQuire, *The Media City: Media, Architecture, and Urban Space* (Thousand Oaks, Calif.: Sage, 2008); Francois Penz and Andong Lu, eds., *Urban Cinematics: Understanding Urban Phenomena through the Moving Image* (London: Intellect, 2011); John David Rhodes and Elena Gorfinkel, eds., *Taking Place: Location and the Moving Image* (Minneapolis: University of

forms of "urban screens," too: scholars have addressed, for instance, the synchronous rise of television and postwar suburbs and the politics of screens in public places.[4] In more recent decades, we've seen a great deal of work on the impact of networked digital media on urban design and urban experience.[5] At the same time, scholars are looking, or listening,

Minnesota Press, 2011); Allen J. Scott, *On Hollywood: The Place, the Industry* (Princeton, N.J.: Princeton University Press, 2005); see also Charlotte Brundson, "The Attractions of the Cinematic City," *Screen* 53, no. 3 (2012): 209–27, for a literature review of "cinematic city" texts.

4. David Heckman, *Small World: Smart Houses and the Dream of the Perfect Day* (Durham, N.C.: Duke University Press, 2008); Shannon Mattern, "Broadcasting Space: China Central Television's New Headquarters," *International Journal of Communication* 2 (2008), http://ijoc.org/ojs/index.php/ijoc/article/view/374/201; Anna McCarthy, *Ambient Television: Visual Culture and Public Space* (Durham, N.C.: Duke University Press, 2001); Scott McQuire, Meredith Martin, and Sabine Niederer, eds., *Urban Screens Reader*, Institute of Network Cultures Reader 5 (Amsterdam: Institute of Network Cultures and Creative Commons, 2009); David Morley, *Home Territories: Media, Mobility, and Identity* (New York: Routledge, 2000); Mitchell Schwarzer, "Television," in *Zoomscape: Architecture in Motion and Media*, 254–305 (New York: Princeton Architectural Press, 2004); Lynn Spigel, *Make Room for TV: Television and the Family Ideal in Postwar America* (Chicago: University of Chicago Press, 1992).

5. M. Christine Boyer, *Cybercities* (New York: Princeton Architectural Press, 1996); Paul Ceruzzi, *Internet Alley: High Technology in Tysons Corner, 1945–2005* (Cambridge, Mass.: MIT Press, 2008); Stephen Graham and Simon Marvin, *Telecommunications and the City: Electronic Spaces, Urban Places* (New York: Routledge, 1996);

back to discern how radio and modern sound technologies affected urban architecture, zoning, and city life.[6]

The sheer number of books and conferences and exhibitions on the "city in photographs," the "cinematic city," and the "digital/smart/sentient city" indicates that most of our attention—at least within the fields of media and design theory and practice—has focused on these modern media technologies' relationships to the city. The *representation* of the city in these modern media continues to be a prominent theme. Furthermore, the emphasis on *imaging* technologies has reinforced an ocularcentric approach, to use historian

Malcolm McCullough, *Digital Ground: Architecture, Pervasive Computing, and Environmental Knowing* (Cambridge, Mass.: MIT Press, 2004); William J. Mitchell, *City of Bits: Space, Place, and the Infobahn* (Cambridge, Mass.: MIT Press, 1996); Mark Shepard, ed., *Sentient City: Ubiquitous Computing, Architecture, and the Future of Urban Space* (Cambridge, Mass.: MIT Press, 2011); Anthony Townsend, *Smart Cities: Big Data, Civic Hackers, and the Quest for a New Utopia* (New York: W. W. Norton, 2013); Mark Wigley, "Network Fever," *Grey Room* 4 (Summer 2001): 82–122.

6. See my "Ear to the Wire." See also Karin Bijsterveld, *Mechanical Sound: Technology, Culture, and Public Problems of Noise in the Twentieth Century* (Cambridge, Mass.: MIT Press, 2008); Steve Goodman, *Sonic Warfare: Sound, Affect, and the Ecology of Fear* (Cambridge, Mass.: MIT Press, 2010); Brian Larkin, *Signal and Noise: Media, Infrastructure, and Urban Culture in Nigeria* (Durham, N.C.: Duke University Press, 2008); Emily Thompson, *The Soundscape of Modernity: Architectural Acoustics and the Culture of Listening in America, 1900–1933* (Cambridge, Mass.: MIT Press, 2004).

Figure 4. Alhambra Inscriptions. Courtesy Luca Quadiro.

Martin Jay's term. There is in many cases an assumption that the mediation of the city began with these modern media. For instance, Eric Gordon, in *The Urban Spectator*, argues that, "from the hand-held camera at the end of the 19th century to the mobile phone at the end of the 20th, the city has *always* been a mediated construct."[7] Yet that "always," I suggest, begins well before the late nineteenth century. As Scott McQuire argues in his *The Media City*, the mediation

7. Eric Gordon, *The Urban Spectator: American Concept-Cities from Kodak to Google* (Hanover, N.H.: Dartmouth College Press, 2010), 2.

of urban experience "has been underway at least since the development of technological images in the context of urban 'modernization' in the mid-19th century."[8] *At least,* indeed. Taking inspiration from Kittler's assertion that "The City *Is* a Medium," and it always has been, I suggest that the "always" of urban mediation extends all the way back to the days of Eridu and Uruk.[9]

Media technologies—particularly their infrastructures—have been embedded in and informing the morphological evolution of our cities since their coming into being. The rise of print, for instance, brought with it new infrastructures for design publishing and education and dramatically influenced design practices, as Mario Carpo has explained.[10] Plus, the emergence of new print forms influenced how people navigated and made sense of their cities. Even to this day, metaphors of the book inform how we "write" and "read" the city. I wrote elsewhere about a "city of books"—a city dedicated to the publication and distribution of books—that, since 2006, has arisen, and conformed to an urban plan

8. McQuire, *Media City*, vii.

9. Kittler, "City Is a Medium," 1996.

10. Mario Carpo, *Architecture in the Age of Printing: Orality, Writing, Typography, and Printed Images in the History of Architectural Theory* (Cambridge, Mass.: MIT Press, 2001). See also Diane Favro, "Meaning and Experience: Urban History from Antiquity to the Early Modern Period," *Journal of the Society of Architectural Historians* 58, no. 3 (1999): 364–73; Rose Marie San Juan, *Rome: A City Out of Print* (Minneapolis: University of Minnesota Press, 2001); Bronwen Wilson, *The World in Venice: Print, the City, and Early Modern Identity* (Buffalo, N.Y.: University of Toronto Press, 2005).

likened to a "landscape script," in the rice paddies north of Seoul, South Korea.[11]

The infrastructures of a chirographic culture—of writing—have also informed, for millennia, how cities took shape. Harold Innis and Lewis Mumford address these relationships, as do archaeologists and art historians like Robert Harrist, who studies Chinese writings in stone, and Brinkley Messick, who examines the history of Islamic architectural inscriptions and their formal parallels in the very "articulation" of urban space.[12] The voice, too, has long been built into urban form. Since the very beginning, cities have been places of public address and conversation, and acoustic considerations have, either by design or by accident, informed design and construction. As I argue elsewhere, we must consider how urban surfaces, volumes, and voids—in cities ranging from ancient Rome to present-day Singapore—have long functioned as sounding boards and resonance chambers for mediation, and as transmission media themselves.[13]

Various anthropologists, archaeologists, and urban his-

11. "Paju Bookcity: The Next Chapter," *Places* (January 2013), https://placesjournal.org/article/paju-bookcity-the-next-chapter/.

12. Robert E. Harrist Jr., *The Landscape of Words: Stone Inscriptions from Early and Medieval China* (Seattle: University of Washington Press, 2008); Harold Innis, *The Bias of Communication* (Buffalo, N.Y.: University of Toronto Press, 1951); Brinkley Messick, *The Calligraphic State: Textual Domination and History in a Muslim Society* (Berkeley: University of California Press, 1993); Lewis Mumford, *The Culture of Cities* (New York: Harcourt Brace Jovanovich, 1938).

13. Mattern, "Ear to the Wire."

torians, like Clifford Geertz, Peter Hall, and Paul Wheatley, posit that the birth of cities is rooted not (or not only) in economics, which is a prevailing theory, but in the need for ceremony and communication.[14] Mumford, author of two grand histories of urbanity, suggests that "what transform[ed] the passive agricultural regimes of the village into the active institutions of the city" was not merely a growth in size or population density or economy but an extension of "the area of local intercourse, that engenders the need for combination and co-operation, communication and communion."[15] That "area of local intercourse" is an infrastructure—a structure that undergirds communication and communion.

14. Clifford Geertz, *Negara: The Theatre State in Nineteenth-Century Bali* (Princeton, N.J.: Princeton University Press, 1980); Peter Hall, *Cities in Civilization* (New York: Pantheon, 1998); Paul Wheatley, *The Pivot of the Four Quarters: A Preliminary Enquiry into the Origins and Character of the Ancient Chinese City* (Chicago: Aldine, 1971).

15. Mumford, *Culture of Cities*, 6.

Infrastructural Entanglements

THE TERM INFRASTRUCTURE was originally used in the mid-1920s to refer to roads, tunnels, and other public works as well as permanent military structures. It was eventually applied more widely to various "man-made systems and processes that function collaboratively and synergistically to produce and distribute a continuous flow of essential goods and services"—systems like transportation, oil and gas production and storage, water supply, emergency services, government services, banking and finance, electrical power, and information and communications.[1] Aspects of these systems—with their asphalt roads, copper wires, and steel pipes—constitute a layered landscape that lends itself to digging into; they leave material residues that we can dig up. Historical communication networks offer artifacts like pneumatic tubes, gutta-percha-coated telegraph cables, old postal roads, technologies for the production and dissemination of

1. President's Commission on Critical Infrastructure Protection, *Critical Foundations: Protecting America's Infrastructures* (Washington, D.C.: President's Commission on Critical Infrastructure Protection, 1997), 3.

early print forms, palimpsests of writing on city walls, and the ruins of ancient amphitheaters. And for the archaeologists of tomorrow, today's wireless technologies will leave behind fiber-optic cables, massive data centers, and piles of e-waste.

Sociologist Susan Leigh Star reminds us that infrastructure also includes intellectual and institutional things, such as measurement standards, naming conventions, classification systems, technical protocols, and bureaucratic forms.[2] Our communication networks have long been shaped by government regulations, international trade agreements, zoning and building codes, various industry standards, and a host of other formal and informal policies and practices. These conceptual infrastructures shape the physical infrastructures of the media city, and vice versa. We might even say that our cities are networks of nested or entangled infrastructures; or, as the saying goes, it's infrastructural "turtles all the way down." An infrastructure, Star says, is "that which runs 'underneath' actual structures[,] . . . that upon which something else rides, or works, a platform of sorts"— but "this common-sense definition begins to unravel when we . . . begin to look at multiple, overlapping and perhaps contradictory infrastructural arrangements. For the railroad engineer, the rails are only infrastructure when she or he is a passenger."[3] Likewise for the systems administrator losing

2. Susan Leigh Star, "The Ethnography of Infrastructure," *American Behavioral Scientist* 43, no. 3 (1999): 377–91.

3. Susan Leigh Star and Geoffrey C. Bowker, "How to Infrastructure," in *Handbook of New Media: Social Shaping and Social Consequences of ICTs*, ed. Leigh A. Lievrouw and Sonia M. Livingstone, 230–44 (Thousand Oaks, Calif.: Sage, 2006).

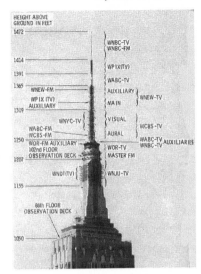

Figure 5. Empire State Building Antenna, by Thomas R. Haskett; originally published in *Broadcast Engineering Magazine* (August 1967). Copyright 2014, New Bay Media. 114277:1114SH.

himself in a game of World of Warcraft. Infrastructure can easily flip between figure and ground; the framing is contextually and situationally defined. Quoting Gregory Bateson, Star suggests that an infrastructure is a "relationship or an infinite regress of relationships. Never a 'thing.'"[4] Infrastructures might have plenty of entangled material elements, but they can never be reduced to an essentializable "thing."

4. Susan Leigh Star and Karen Ruhleder, "Steps toward an Ecology of Infrastructure: Complex Problems in Design and Access for Large-Scale Collaborative Systems," in *Proceedings of the 1994 ACM Conference on Computer Supported Cooperative Work* (New York: Association for Computing Machinery Press, 1994), 246; Gregory Bateson, *Steps to an Ecology of Mind* (Chicago: University of Chicago Press, 1972), 246.

Plus, some communication infrastructures offer archaeologists very few things to hit with a shovel. How does one dig into a form of mediation that seemingly has no physical form?[5] Consider the "sonic city"—the city of radio waves and public address and everyday conversation. Its "artifacts" are primarily sonic, and in most cases, their echoes have long since faded. Yet the material spaces in which those echoes once reverberated can offer invaluable clues about how cities (re-) sounded. It's particularly in cases like these where media and network archaeologists can benefit from the work of archaeologists proper; we can learn about our media networks by excavating their urban contexts. Archaeology and its subfield of archeoacoustics, along with architectural and urban history and allied fields, can help us to understand, for instance, the ways in which radio and sound waves have interacted with, and even shaped, the material city—how our urban surfaces, volumes, and voids have functioned as sounding boards, resonance chambers, and transmission media. What we ultimately find is that our media histories are deeply "networked" with our urban and architectural histories and that, in many cases, these cultural and technological forms are mutually constructed.

We'll also discover that there are more epistemological and historiographic resonances between media and network archaeology, and archaeology proper, than we might expect (and perhaps we can even add some mutual political goals,

5. Much of the following is drawn from my "Ear to the Wire" and my "Deep Time of Media Infrastructure."

including redressing the "great man" and colonialist histories of some of these fields of study). While media archaeology seeks to offer alternatives to canonized historical media narratives and the "idea of inexorable, quasi-natural, technical progress," the familiar notion of archaeological "stratification" seems to make manifest the very idea of layered epochs of "progress."[6] Yet archaeologists have challenged the stratification model, arguing that it "wraps blocks of linear temporality up into periods placed into neatly stacked boxes," separated by "arbitrary divisions."[7] Christopher Witmore suggests that the metaphor of the palimpsest presents similar conceptual problems: historical layers aren't simply "written, erased, and rewritten"; instead, there are plenty of "points of connection, proximity and action between various pasts."[8] Many archaeologists (some drawing inspiration from Bergson, Deleuze, Serres, Barad, etc.) have embraced the notion of temporal entanglement. If we reject the idea that there are stratified epochs of "revolution"-based history, with new developments eradicating old systems, we need to rethink how the archaeological object—whether an ancient urn or a network of fiber-optic cable—is conceived. Seemingly "modern" things, Witmore says, are "really [just] gatherings of achievements from various times and numerous

6. Siegfried Zielinski, *Deep Time of the Media: Toward an Archaeology of Hearing and Seeing by Technical Means* (Cambridge, Mass.: MIT Press, 2006), 3.

7. Christopher L. Witmore, "Symmetrical Archaeology: Excerpts of a Manifesto," *World Archaeology* 39, no. 4 (2007): 555–56.

8. Ibid., 556.

places."[9] (The following image shows the myriad discoveries and inventions that had to come before the iPhone for such a device even to be thinkable.) Knowing the modern media city thus requires that we trace the technologies, architectures, economies, social practices, and so on, that are tangled up in its production. And appreciating the entanglement of these histories will help us to move forward, into the future, in a more critical fashion.

These highly theoretical models actually take shape and become physical in our urban infrastructural landscapes. In many cases, our older infrastructures have lain the foundation for our modern-day systems (as per the technological and economic principle of "path dependency"), but the "old" systems—those we might regard as buried on the "lower strata"—are also very much alive in, and continuing to shape, the contemporary city. These historical media are, like Raymond Williams's category of the "residual," "formed in the past, but . . . still active in the cultural process, not only and *often* not at *all* as an element of the past, but as an effective element of the present."[10]

What's more, these various systems have distinctive temporalities and evolutionary paths; they don't all "progress" at a standard rate. Through excavation we can assess the lifespans of media networks and ascertain when "old" infrastructures leak into new-media landscapes, when media of different epochs are layered palimpsestically, or when new

9. Ibid., 558.
10. Raymond Williams, *Marxism and Literature* (New York: Oxford University Press, 1977), 122.

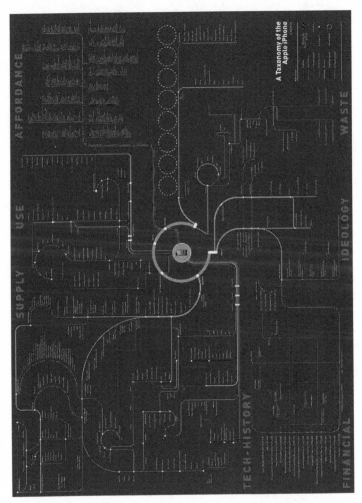

Figure 6. iPhone Genealogy. From Benjamin J. Millen, *Critical Wayfinding, or a Psycho Spatial Model for Critical Design,* MDes thesis, University of Calgary Faculty of Environmental Design, 2009.

urban media remediate their predecessors.[11] Richard John, who's written histories of American telecommunications and the postal system, has found that the infrastructures he's studied were "complementary rather than mutually exclusive. Telegraphy supplemented mail delivery, and telephony supplemented telegraphy, without rendering either mail delivery or telegraphy obsolete."[12] Though the electronic and digital ages have dealt serious blows to both the post and telegraphy, new media need not necessarily obsolesce the old; we'll likely still listen to the radio and scratch out handwritten notes in our "sentient cities" of tomorrow,

11. My work thus responds to Alan Liu's call, in his keynote at the Network Archaeology conference at Miami University in spring 2012, for a "media-archaeological method . . . for capturing such networks of combined past and present—oral, written, print, analog, and/or digital." Liu, "Remembering Networks: Agrippa, RoSE, and Network Archaeology," presented at the Network Archaeology Conference, Miami University, Oxford, Ohio, April 21, 2012. See OPSYS/Alexandra Gauzza's "Infrastructure Lifespans" timeline for the Harvard Graduate School of Design "Landscape Futures" event; the graphic is far too intricate to reproduce in print: http://m. ammoth.us/blog/wp-content/uploads/2012/03/Harvard-GSD_Landscape-Infrastructure-Symposium_March-23-24-2012_Poster-Program-s-2.jpg.

12. Richard R. John, "Recasting the Information Infrastructure for the Industrial Age," in *A Nation Transformed: How Information Has Shaped the United States from Colonial Times to the Present,* ed. Alfred D. Chandler Jr. and James W. Cortada (New York: Oxford University Press, 2000), 56. See Derek Watkins's animated visualization of the spread of U.S. post offices: http://vimeo.com/27376376.

for instance. Various networks also provide material support for one another. Geographers Stephen Graham and Simon Marvin write that "because of the costs of developing new telecommunications networks," for instance, "all efforts are made to string optic fibers through water, gas, and sewage ducts; [and] *between* cities, existing railway, road, and water-way routes are often used."[13]

Although the notion of temporal entanglement has been embraced within media studies and is gaining purchase within archaeology—and though media and network archaeologists have managed to question the notion of "inexorable progress" by excavating our new-media technologies' roots in the nineteenth, and occasionally the eighteenth, century—most existing media excavation work doesn't offer a terribly deep historical perspective. Another benefit of infusing media and network archaeology with archaeology proper is that, once equipped with theoretical trowels, we can dig much deeper. Archaeology proper, along with architectural and urban history and related fields, provides many tools for media and network archaeologists to engage, through multiple senses, the deep time of urban mediation.[14]

Equally significantly, archaeology promotes a more global

13. Graham and Marvin, *Telecommunications and the City*, 329.
14. Rosalind Williams, in her study of subterranean technologies (mines, subways, sewers, etc.), links the notion of "deep time" to Marx's "subsurface history," Freud's subconscious, and structuralism's "deep structures." Williams, *Notes on the Underground: An Essay on Technology, Society, and the Imagination*, new ed. (Cambridge, Mass.: MIT Press, 2008).

view. The "media city" is frequently conflated with the "global city," which is global primarily in that it is a privileged central hub in overlapping international networks.[15] Consequently, much work on the media city focuses on global capitals like New York, Paris, Berlin, London, and Tokyo. Although there is still much insight about urban mediation to be excavated at these sites, and though some scholars have explored areas of the Global South and other underexplored regions of the world, we can do more to look beyond the heavily networked cities that dominate the existing research.[16] By expanding the geographic focus of our study of urban mediation, we can show that infrastructural networks reach parts of the globe that are rarely on our radar and that the network manifests itself differently in different cities. Highlighting this variation can help us to better appreciate the politics of the media city, too—the uneven spread of networks and access to infrastructurally distributed resources, uneven rates of technological development and commitment to maintenance, and diverse systems of ownership and control.

15. Saskia Sassen, *The Global City: New York, London, Tokyo* (Princeton, N.J.: Princeton University Press, 1991).

16. See Larkin, *Signal and Noise*; Lisa Parks, *Mixed Signals: Media Infrastructures and Cultural Geographies* (manuscript in progress); Anja Schwarz and Lars Eckstein, *Postcolonial Piracy: Media Distribution and Cultural Production in the Global South* (London: Bloomsbury, 2014); Ravi Sundaram, *Pirate Modernity: Delhi's Media Urbanism* (New York: Routledge, 2010); and Helga Tawil-Souri's work on media infrastructures in Israel and Palestine.

Figure 7. Screenshot from Bangalore Telecom Infrastructure Map. Metamap, Centre Régional Information Jeunesse, http://bangalore.metamap.fr/.

We can see here one node in a citizen-made map of telecom infrastructures in Bangalore. The map's creators describe how the map, and others like it in the Subjective Cartography series, were made:

> We build our subjective maps by combining different methods: photography, film, and sound recording; we use home-made tools and sensors to explore the visible and invisible electromagnetic city; we make measurements by taking water from street vendors and performing DIY biological analysis (with webcams made into microscopes); we adopt psycho-geographical approaches in exploring territory . . . ; we produce expressions of personal subjectivity; and we have meetings with experts and witnesses.

This mention of media in multiple modalities leads us into our next section.

Multisensory Methods

MEDIA ARCHAEOLOGISTS like Kittler and Wolfgang Ernst, and media historians like Lisa Gitelman, advise us to consider the specific material natures of our historical records and artifacts.[1] If we think of our cities themselves as historical media, or archaeological artifacts embodying their entangled temporalities of evolution, we have to acknowledge that they're not just historical texts to be read or artifacts to be gazed upon.[2] They can also serve as resonance chambers in which we hear echoes of conversations and

1. Likewise, John Durham Peters suggested that astronomy and geology are both forms of media study in that they rely on the reading of texts that are far removed from their place and time of origin. As Kittler and Ernst argue, these "texts cannot be interpreted apart from an interpretation of the processes that produced them." Astronomy and geology thus "necessarily study not only content, but signal and channel properties as well." Peters, "Space, Time, and Communication Theory."

2. We might say that our cities are themselves historical media, or archaeological artifacts embodying their entangled temporalities of evolution: "Cities are a product of time. They are the molds in which men's lifetimes have cooled and congealed, giving lasting shape, by way

oratory and radio broadcasts from the past. They're textural environments in which we feel traces of architectural inscriptions and centuries' worth of public notices affixed to building facades, and where we shake with the vibrations of loud sonic media—today, a booming subwoofer in a passing car, centuries ago, the village bells. And that static we sometimes feel in the air on cold, dry days is the same electromagnetic activity that convinced early experimenters that the "ether" might support wireless communication. We can even detect olfactory clues of the city's mediation; walking past a paper recycling plant in the Dumbo neighborhood of Brooklyn, or through a printing district in Seoul, reminds us that our historical publishing centers also smelled of ink and paper.

Though there has, over the past two decades, been some excellent work in sonic history and the sounds of historical sites, much existing work on the media city presents it as a visual entity, and the urban dweller as first and foremost a spectator—a subject position that implies a particular, limited politics of engagement with the city.[3] I hope to redress—in this short book, and in the larger study that

---

of art, to moments that would otherwise vanish with the living and leave no means of renewal or wider participation behind them. In the city, time becomes visible: buildings and monuments and public ways, more open than the written record, more subject to the gaze of many men than the scattered artifacts of the countryside, leave an imprint upon the minds even of the ignorant or the indifferent." Mumford, *Culture of Cities*, 4.

3. I discuss this ocularcentrism, and provide an overview of texts and creative projects that redress this visual emphasis, in "Silent, Invis-

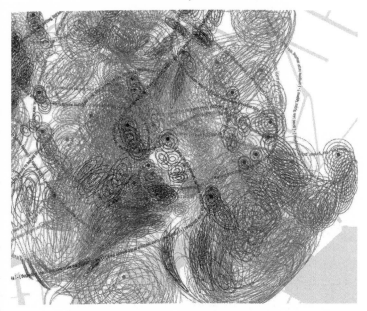

Figure 8. *Smellmap: Amsterdam* (detail), 2014, Kate McLean. Digital print. 46 in. × 46 in. Designer's Collection, United Kingdom.

this Forerunner fore*shadows*—both the limited historical and sensory scope of this existing work by demonstrating the copresence of media from myriad epochs and by depicting cities past and present as spaces that are simultaneously aural, graphic, textual, electroacoustic, digital, and haptic. Clues in any one of these sensory modes might

ible City: Mediating Urban Experience for the *Other* Senses," in *Mediacity: Situations, Practices, and Encounters,* ed. Frank Eckardt et al., 155–76 (Berlin: Frank and Timme, 2009).

offer insights into other registers. Emily Thompson, in *The Soundscape of Modernity*, acknowledges that "everyday sounds" from the early twentieth century, her period of study, "are virtually always lost to the historian, who must necessarily turn to textual descriptions and silent photographs to elicit the lost reverberations of the past."[4] In his *The Acoustic World of Early Modern England*, Bruce R. Smith "assembled evidence from travelers' accounts, estate maps, letters, diaries, sermons, plays, poems, fictional narratives, ballads from oral tradition, and architectural remains, and interpreted that evidence in relation to sixteenth- and seventeenth-century ideas about sound and the human body, and in light of modern principles of acoustic ecology, psychoacoustics, architectural acoustics, and socio-linguistics."[5] Of course we can't know precisely how the denizens of early modern England heard the cries of street barkers, or how the citizens of ancient Rome heard a public address in the forum; there's necessarily some speculation involved in piecing together the sensory dimensions of urban and media history. Architectural historian Diane Favro and classicist Christopher Johanson acknowledge that creating a model of an "entire urban space," and imaging its textures and colors and acoustic properties, "requires hypotheses and assumptions about many unknown aspects."[6] Such

4. Thompson, *Soundscape of Modernity*, 205.

5. Bruce R. Smith, "How Sound Is Sound History? A Response to Mark Smith," *Journal of the Historical Society* 2 (2002): 306–15.

6. Diane Favro and Christopher Johanson, "Death in Motion: Funeral Processions in the Roman Forum," *Journal of the Society of*

indeterminacy "is unpalatable to many scholars, but especially to archaeologists, who are trained to appreciate accuracy, not speculation."

But speculative methods do at least allow us to acknowledge our media cities as multisensory and to appreciate that these myriad sensory registers are integral to mediation. Speculative models allow us to imagine, if not posit definitive claims regarding, what our historical media cities looked, sounded, and felt like—and how urban politics might have been exercised through these empirical and affective registers. Urban and architectural historians and archaeologists have much methodological insight to offer in this endeavor—in large part because they already appreciate what a historical and material understanding of media and infrastructure can offer to archaeology proper. In their *Archaeology: The Discipline of Things*, Bjørnar Olsen, Michael Shanks, Timothy Webmoor, and Christopher Witmore speak of

> making manifest the past (or, crucially . . . allow[ing] the past to manifest itself) in its traces through practices and performances (writing, corresponding, visiting, touring, mapping, pacing, debating), artifacts (letter, notebook, manuscript, printed book, pamphlet, map, plan, plaster cast, model), instruments (pen, paint brushes, rule, Claude Glass, camera lucida, surveying instruments, boots, wheeled transport, spades, shovels,

---

Architectural Historians 69, no. 1 (2010): 12–13. See RomeLab at the UCLA Experiential Technologies Center: http://etc.ucla.edu/research/projects/romelab/.

buckets), systems and standards (taxonomy, itinerary, grid), authorized algorithms (the new philology, legal witnessing), dreams and design (... of a nation's identity, of personal achievement). Making manifest came through manifold articulations.[7]

Olsen and his colleagues regard these various disciplinary infrastructures—technologies, instruments, protocols, and standards—as modes of engaging with and manifesting the past. Different tools for record keeping and representation manifest different aspects of that past, including those ineffable qualities that don't readily lend themselves to "accurate," standardized formats of representation. Witmore argues that using a mixture of media—field recordings, photographs, maps, and so on—can allow archaeologists to "translate something of the sensory, physical presence of the material past."[8]

7. Olsen et al., *Archaeology: The Discipline of Things*, 93.
8. Witmore, "Symmetrical Archaeology," 554. I also address multisensorial methods for "experiencing" infrastructure in my "Infrastructural Tourism," *Places* (July 2013), https://placesjournal.org/article/infrastructural-tourism/.

Deep Mapping
the Media City

EVEN THOSE FIELDS that are more interested in the futures of our landscapes than in their pasts recognize the importance of developing appropriate tools for investigating and representing the sensory, physical presence of history. Because architects, landscape architects, and engineers sometimes find themselves building on unstable ground or on top of existing infrastructure—over railbeds, brown fields, or landfills, for example—they need to be aware of "complex site dynamics."[1] Landscape architects Stephanie Carlisle and Nicholas Pavzner propose that their fellow designers need new tools, beyond the traditional plans and perspectives, that allow them to better deal with deep structures and dynamic forces. To work with "deep urbanism," which regards the city as a "complex system composed of interconnected layers of social and biogeochemical processes," designers need the "deep section." The deep section

1. Stephanie Carlisle and Nicholas Pavzner, "The Performative Ground: Rediscovering the Deep Section," *Landscape Urbanism* (Spring 2012), http://scenariojournal.com/article/the-performative-ground/.

is a representational tool that "brings infrastructure . . . to the forefront, expanding our understanding of the pre-conditions of projects and the boundaries of [designers' potential] interventions." By presenting multiple infrastructures simultaneously, the deep section allows designers to explore them in relation to one another and to imagine how our future systems could correspond to the paths laid out by their predecessors.

Of course there are myriad artists and media makers and writers—Dziga Vertov, Walter Benjamin, Constant Nieuwenhuys and the Situationists, Alighiero Boetti, Lize Mogel and Alexis Bhagat, Rebecca Solnit, Joyce Kozloff, and Julie Mehretu among them—who discerned a similar need for new tools and strategies to represent modern spaces, and the modern city in particular. The "literary montage" form of Benjamin's *Arcades Project*, and the reader's experience in engaging with it, are regarded as "city-like"; its textual passages resemble, in their pace and structure, the passages of urban exhibition halls, arcades, and train stations.[2] Cartographers and geographers, too, have experimented with various critical, counter-, and radical cartographic approaches, including indigenous mapping, sensory mapping, and the collaborative development of OpenStreetMap, an open-source alternative to Google Earth.[3] These approaches

2. Graeme Gilloch, *Myth and Metropolis: Walter Benjamin and the City* (Malden, Mass.: Polity Press, 1997).

3. See Jeremy W. Crampton and John Krygier, "An Introduction to Critical Cartography," *ACME: An International e-Journal for Critical Geographies* 4, no. 1 (2006): 11–33; John Pickles, *A History of Spaces: Cartographic Reason, Mapping and the Geo-Coded World*

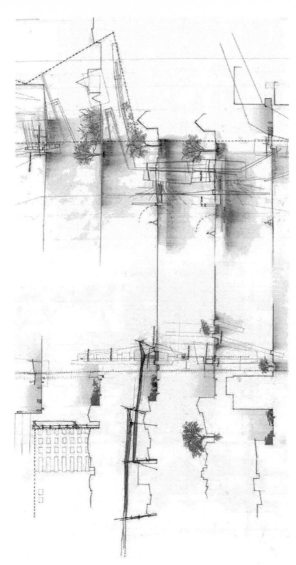

Figure 9. Sequential Sections. From *Filter/Collector: Anchoring the Edge in Mumbai's Maidans*. Image by Nicholas Pevzner. Originally published in *Scenario Journal*.

aim to illuminate the unavoidably subjective and political aspects of mapping and to provide alternatives to hegemonic, authoritative—and often naturalized and reified—approaches to cartography.

Today's urban form is perhaps best expressed not through a two-dimensional map but via the remixed iPod playlist, the database documentary, and a live feed of data accessible via the smartphone. Archaeologists have also traditionally been early adopters and developers of new technologies, from photographs to remote sensing, for surveying and annotating their fields of study. Favro and Johanson are among those studying the ancient past who are experimenting with new technologies.[4] They're interested in the "symbiotic exchange" between "urban form" and "kinetic ceremonies," particularly the funeral procession, in ancient Rome; in short, they wonder how the city functions as an infrastructure for such ceremonial, and highly mediated, events. They regard digital modeling as particularly well suited to

---

(New York: Routledge, 2004); Nancy Peluso, "Whose Woods Are These? Counter-Mapping Forest Territories in Kalimantan, Indonesia," *Antipode* 4, no. 27 (1995): 383–406; David Pinder, "Subverting Cartography: The Situationists and Maps of the City," *Environment and Planning A* 28 (1996): 405–27; Bill Rankin, "Radical Cartography," http://www.radicalcartography.net/; Denis Wood, *The Power of Maps* (New York: Guilford Press, 1992). We explore many of these critical cartographic approaches, as well as many examples of cartographic art, in my Urban Media Archaeology graduate studio course, which I've taught at the New School since 2010.

4. See their RomeLab at the UCLA Experiential Technologies Center: http://etc.ucla.edu/research/projects/romelab/.

Figure 10. Schematic view of the Roman Forum. Model copyright and courtesy of the Regents of the University of California, Christopher Johanson, and the Experiential Technologies Center [ETC], UCLA.

getting at all those ineffable dimensions of the city—"its sights, movement, sounds, and smells," all of which are integral dimensions to the politics of pageantry, and broader practices of governmentality—that are hard to capture in a sketch, drawing, or physical model:[5]

> Digital technologies have made possible the fashioning of more dynamic and flexible depictions of ancient spaces . . . , all readily linked to metadata that documents the level of accuracy of

5. Favro and Johanson, "Death in Motion," 15.

restored components. . . . A rich range of sensorial stimuli can be added to kinetic viewing to shape more robust recreations of the original environmental experience. Depictions of actual times of day, year, and century reaffirm the essential temporal aspects. . . . Various experimental scenarios can be presented to ascertain the impact of alternative reconstructions, climatic conditions, and hypothetically distributed ephemera.

But because, they say, archaeologists are generally averse to speculation, it's important to offer context for these experimental and hypothetical dimensions of the model. "Every sensorial layer requires a method of citation and analysis, and a large measure of scholarly caution. How can it be proved that ancients experienced light in the same way as moderns? How does one add scholarly rigor to the simulation of smell or sound?"[6]

What kind of map or model can accommodate this integration of spatial and temporal and sensory dynamics, acknowledge that various rendered elements reflect varying degrees of certainty (and that some are entirely speculative)—and make clear that the urban substrate in which all those forces converge was itself shaped through a long period of evolution?[7] What kind of map can show networks entangled with networks, confirming Kittler's observation that "a city is not a flattenable graph"?

For mapping deep time, maybe we need a deep map. The

6. Ibid., 16.

7. See Michele Tucci and Alberto Giordano, "Positional Accuracy, Positional Uncertainty, and Feature Change Detection in Historical Maps," *Computers, Environment, and Urban Analysis* 35, no. 6 (2011): 452–563.

deep map, as archaeologists Mike Pearson and Michael Shanks explain, "attempts to record and represent the grain and patina of place through juxtapositions and interpenetrations of the historical and the contemporary, the political and the poetic, the discursive and the sensual; the conflation of oral testimony, anthology, memoir, biography, natural history and everything you might ever want to say about a place."[8] Though Pearson's and Shanks's list of ingredients is rather literary, we can also layer in GIS and empirical data and satellite images, thus juxtaposing qualitative and quantitative conceptions of space, or balancing out GIS's seeming precision with the relative fuzziness of humanistic data.[9] Fellow archaeologist Cliff McLucas adds that deep maps are characterized not only by their layering of different media or registers but also by their "engagement of both the insider and outsider," "the official and the unofficial"—much like the Subjective Cartographies project we looked at earlier.[10] Deep maps don't claim to be authoritative or objective; to

8. Mike Pearson and Michael Shanks, *Theatre/Archaeology* (New York: Routledge, 2001), 64–65. See also Todd Presner, David Shepard, and Yoh Kawano, *HyperCities: Thick Mapping in the Digital Humanities* (Cambridge, Mass.: Harvard University Press, 2014), and David Bodenhamer, John Corrigan, and Trevor M. Harris, eds., *Deep Maps and Spatial Narratives* (Bloomington: Indiana University Press, forthcoming).

9. See David J. Bodenhamer, "The Potential of the Spatial Humanities," in *The Spatial Humanities: GIS and the Future of Humanities Scholarship,* ed. David Bodenhamer, John Corrigan, and Trevor M. Harris, 14–30 (Bloomington: Indiana University Press, 2010).

10. Cliff McLucas, "Deep Mapping," http://metamedia.stanford.edu/~mshanks/projects/deep-mapping.html.

the contrary, they're intentionally "fragile and temporary"—always evolving and evading stable representation, just like our media and the cities they inhabit and shape.

Users' engagement with a deep map of the media city can be similarly dynamic; users can open or close, and turn on or off, different layers to explore various forces and networks in relation to one another. We can see this functionality in my colleague Brian McGrath's *Manhattan Timeformations*,[11] an interactive map of dynamic urban systems, which was rather pathbreaking when it was launched in 2000. We can toggle on and off layers for highways, subways, rails, monuments and parks, and landfill, for instance, and filter by historic period. The map offers additional interactive features that allow us to explore our cities' growth and infrastructural development from multiple vantage points—as if we were looking at Manhattan from Brooklyn or from an approach on the Staten Island Ferry. These features aren't merely gratuitous acrobatics, similar to those we find in most nausea-inducing Prezi presentations; instead, they provide methodological and epistemological value, affording us an opportunity to see historical and spatial patterns in development and to identify pockets of exclusion.

Users of deep, interactive maps can also zoom in to examine cities and their infrastructures at various scales and to compare them in different geographic regions. Such comparisons can help to disabuse us of the classic deterministic view of infrastructure, which Graham and Marvin describe in *Splintering Urbanism* as the assumption that

11. http://www.skyscraper.org/timeformations/intro.html.

new networked systems create new urban *forms* in their image.[12] Zooming in and out also reveals that infrastructures operate, and interlink, at different scales, "from the body to the globe."[13] The interlinking or entanglement of infrastructures and temporalities is another key dimension that a deep map can reveal.[14] What we see in the following, however, is a very simple map—by map theorist and experimental cartographer Denis Wood—that also conveys this rather messy overlapping of scales: newspaper delivery zones, police zones, garbage pickup zones, planning zones, state election districts, school zones.

Maps can also help us identify patterns of concentration, segmentation, or uneven distribution of (or access to) infrastructures. Geographer Karen Bakker argues, contra Graham and Marvin, that global infrastructures aren't "splintering" but are inherently "splintered"; islands of access within seas of exclusion are the norm in many parts of the developing (and even developed) world, where governments don't

12. Stephen Graham and Simon Marvin, eds., *Splintering Urbanism: Networked Infrastructures, Technological Mobilities, and the Urban Condition* (New York: Routledge, 2001), 21.

13. Ibid., 8.

14. As Graham notes, "only very rarely do single infrastructure networks develop in isolation from changes in others. By far the most common situation is where urban landscapes and processes become remodeled and reconstituted based on their complex articulations with a variety of superimposed transport, communications, energy and water infrastructures.... What is the Internet without electricity? Or the contemporary highway without the mobile phone?" Stephen Graham, "Introduction: Cities and Infrastructure Networks," *International Journal of Urban and Regional Research* 24, no. 1 (2000): 114.

Figure 11. "Nesting." From Denis Wood, *Everything Sings: Maps for a Narrative Atlas,* 2nd ed. (Siglio, 2013).

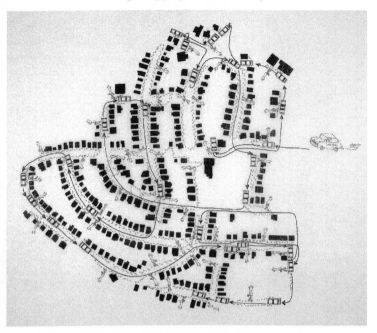

Figure 12. "Mailman." From Denis Wood, *Everything Sings: Maps for a Narrative Atlas,* 2nd ed. (Siglio, 2013).

provide universal access to public services.[15] The NYTE worked with MIT's Senseable City Lab to visualize telecom activity, and we can see here the global flows and fallows.

Rahul Mehrota, describing contemporary Indian cities, distinguishes between the "Static City," a place of formal,

15. Karen Bakker, "Splintered Urbanisms: Water, Urban Infrastructure, and the Modern Social Imaginary," in *Urban Constellations*, ed. Matthew Gandy (Berlin: GmbH, 2011), 62–64.

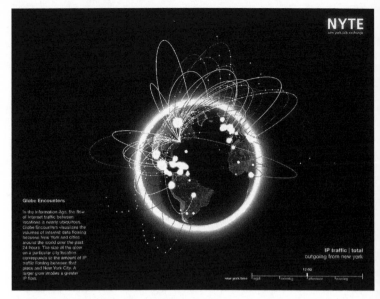

Figure 13. NYTE "Globe Encounters." Courtesy the MIT Senseable City Lab.

permanent, and often monumental structures of concrete, steel, and brick, and the "Kinetic City," a place of informal, dynamic, incremental, and temporary development, where much is built from recycled materials: scrap metal, waste wood, plastic sheets, reclaimed wires and cables.[16] Bakker suggests that we might see the construction of makeshift,

16. Rahul Mehrotra, "Negotiating the Static and Kinetic Cities: The Emergent Urbanism of Mumbai," in *Other Cities, Other Worlds: Urban Imaginaries in a Globalizing Age*, ed. Andreas Huyssen, 205–18 (Durham, N.C.: Duke University Press, 2008).

jury-rigged, or pirated structures, or the use of biopower—of people themselves as links in a disconnected network—as a form of "intense, often undocumented innovation" (and as evidence of political struggle).[17] The deep map of these two intertwined cities—the static and kinetic—could allow us to represent how formal, state-implemented or commercial infrastructures—mapped via official GIS data—engage with informal infrastructures, which we might map via oral testimony and ethnographic photography and video. There is much to be gained by putting these two cartographic techniques and subjects in relation to one another. For instance, the Kinetic City, Mehrota says, is typically that which is "excluded from the spaces of global flows," but it has the potential to force the Static City to "re-engage itself," to reconsider its politics, and perhaps to wonder what it might learn from its Kinetic counterpart.[18]

Another innovative mapping project sought to make sense of jury-rigged biotechnical infrastructures and living patterns in Hong Kong, described as "a city without ground." "This is true," the map makers write, "both physically ([because it's] built on steep slopes, the city has no ground plane) and culturally ([in that] there is no concept of ground). Density obliterates figure-ground in the city."[19] Adam Frampton, Jonathan Solomon, and Clara Wong

17. Bakker, "Splintered Urbanisms," 64; AbdouMaliq Simone, "People as Infrastructure: Intersecting Fragments in Johannesburg," *Public Culture* 16, no. 3 (2004): 407–29.

18. Mehrota, "Negotiating the Static and Kinetic Cities," 207, 216.

19. *Cities without Ground*, http://www.citieswithoutground.com/.

look at the layered topography of Hong Kong, known for its entangled—and partly unplanned—systems of walkways, tunnels, ramps, and passageways. The assemblage, the authors write, is the "result of a combination of top-down planning and bottom-up solutions, a unique collaboration between pragmatic thinking and comprehensive master-planning."

Cities without Ground shows many of the 3-D circulation routes that inhabitants have created through the city. As the authors explain, these maps show that "this continuous network, and the microclimates of temperature, humidity, noise

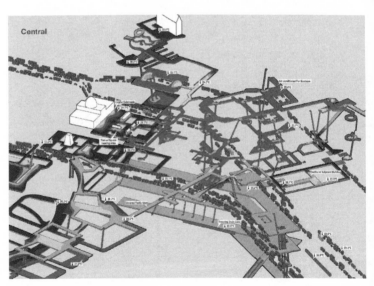

Figure 14. *Cities without Ground* spread depicting transit routes determined by temperature. Image by Adam Frampton, Jonathan D. Solomon, and Clara Wong.

and smell which differentiate it, constitute an entirely new form of urban spatial hierarchy. The relation between shopping malls and air temperature, for instance, suggests architectural implications in circulation—differentiating spaces where pedestrians eagerly flow or make efforts to avoid, where people stop and linger or where smokers gather."

One of the *Cities without Ground* maps depicts West Kowloon—and just a few months after the book's publication was the twentieth anniversary of an important event in this area: the demolition of Kowloon Walled City, a notorious hyperdense and largely ungoverned settlement. Such informal conditions typically can't be discerned via GPS or official maps. Informal infrastructures are uncovered instead through on-the-ground fieldwork, interviews, participant observation, and other qualitative methods we'd typically apply in creating a deep map. We see this in the Financing Small Cities initiative, which trained researchers to fan out into the town of Srirangapatna, India, to gather data on residents' access to infrastructure. Their maps—which you can see online (http://financingcities.ifmr.co.in/blog/2012/12/10/data-analytics/), are rather simple data visualizations, but the stories and observations the team gathered in the field could've been organized into a deep map, again like the Subjective Cartography project.

Here the team had to "go to the source" and ask the residents themselves about their access to resources. As Graham reminds us, looking at an "official" network map—from a telecom or publishing company, for instance—can tell us only so much about individuals' *access* along routes of a network; "one can be physically on top of an access point to

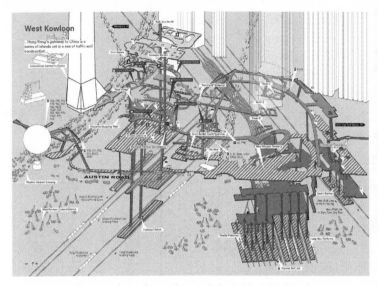

Figure 15. *Cities without Ground* spread depicting West Kowloon.
Image by Adam Frampton, Jonathan D. Solomon, and Clara Wong.

an infrastructure network whilst, at the same time, being
'infinitely' excluded from it"—just as one can live right
beside an interstate, while the closest on- and off-ramps are
miles away.[20] Lisa Parks, whose pioneering work focuses on
both formal and informal satellite infrastructures, advocates
that, in using official network or GIS-based maps, we have
to "trust but verify."[21] Some maps, she acknowledges, are

20. Stephen Graham, "Introduction: Cities and Infrastructure Networks," *International Journal of Urban and Regional Research* 24,
no. 1 (2000): 116.

21. Lisa Parks, Signal Traffic Workshop, University of California
at Santa Barbara, June 2, 2011.

intentionally obscure, particularly when their creators have reason to worry about their networks' security.[22] Such verification strategies include potholing, which involves digging small holes to check for underground utilities, and ground truthing, or gathering data in the field to corroborate or challenge remotely sensed or government- or corporate-issued data. That's how Michael Chen and Justin Snider's cell phone infrastructure map, which we saw earlier, was generated—by collecting official data, then walking the streets, confirming and documenting that cell phone antennae were where the various government agencies and corporations said they were.[23]

Mapping both static *and kinetic* infrastructures can reveal how they evolve in tandem, sometimes overlapping, sometimes diverging; how they emerge via top-down, state-sponsored or organic, resident-driven efforts; and how these different systems are often divided by class or geography. Mehrota suggests that the copresence of diverse networks that morph over time inspires us to think of the city not as a "grand vision" but as a "grant adjustment." Mapping these official and informal systems can help to reveal the "elastic

22. Nicholas Jackson, "15 High-Profile Sites That Google Doesn't Want You to See," *The Atlantic Tech* (June 21, 2011), http://www .theatlantic.com/technology/archive/2011/06/15-high-profile-sites-that-google-doesnt-want-you-to-see/240766/.

23. Then again, some places have no network maps to check our field-derived data *against*. Marko Peljhan has constructed telecommunication infrastructures in the Arctic, a region with "little infrastructure beyond human networks"; thus oral history has become a central methodology in constructing both his network and the map of it.

urban condition," allowing comparison of networks and cities over time, perhaps all the way back into deep time. The timeline—which offers the ability to map urban and technological evolution across time—is another great advantage of interactive mapping, and *deep* mapping only enhances our understanding of urban and technological temporality by revealing the presence of multiple histories.

In closing, I want to tour briefly through just a few more in-progress (or possibly stalled) interactive mapping projects that have the potential either to add to our set of cartographic methodological tools or to demonstrate the challenges (if not impossibility) of translating nuanced understandings of cultural history into digital cartographic form. First, there's Pleiades,[24] a "community-built gazeteer" and map of ancient places, which currently includes some plotted points—including markers, on ancient roadways— that pertain to the "deep time" of the mediated city. Then there's Hypercities,[25] a project that hypothetically allows for an exploration of layered temporalities but whose design challenges—including particularly its organization into nonintuitive "collections," and the lack of unique URLs for plotted data, which prevents users from linking back to individual items posted to the map—significantly limit its functionality. Nicole Starosielski has subverted many cartographic conventions in developing a map of undersea cables to accompany her forthcoming book on the topic. She and designer Eric Loyer have been custom designing a platform

24. http://pleiades.stoa.org/home.
25. http://www.hypercities.com/.

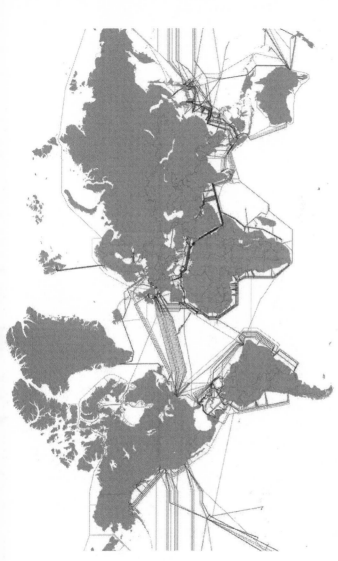

Figure 16. Undersea cable map. From TeleGeography, http://www.submarinecablemap.com/.

that allows users to explore the map though themes or stories, by place, or via the networks traced on the map.

And since 2010, the graduate students in Urban Media Archaeology studio have been creating maps of historical urban media networks using the Urban Research Toolkit (URT), a (now "hibernating") mapping platform that my colleagues in Parsons the New School for Design created in collaboration with me—partly in *response* to the methodological needs of my class. URT was built entirely using open-source technology and was meant to allow users to geolocate archival or self-generated data in myriad formats, and to *contextualize* that data within an argument or story. Over the four years I taught the class, students have mapped the geography of newspaper printing and delivery; the migration of media company headquarters throughout Manhattan from the late nineteenth through the early twenty-first centuries; the disappearance of movie theaters in Greenpoint, Brooklyn; carrier pigeon geographic history; the entwined histories of department stores and radio stations; the history of zines and small-publishing distribution in the East Village of the 1970s; the geography of telephone switching stations; the rise and fall of independent bookstores; and numerous other fascinating histories.

Our platform was not without its limitations, and our process was not without its frustrations. But the very messiness of the mapping practice allowed our students to see *inside* the software development process and to appreciate the friction between various temporalities: they were

Figure 17. Student projects from my Urban Media Archaeology graduate studio.

ARCHITECTURE OF MEDIA

Created by JULIANA PEREIRA *NOVEMBER 28th 2012*

DESCRIPTION

For this Urban Media Archaeology project, I decided to investigate the architecture of a handful of media publishers in New York City. I am intrigued by how architecture can mediate a corporate image, subtly by its style and also its location. In examining different buildings and locations from the mid-nineteenth century through the present day, I hope to try and understand the choices that newspaper and media companies have made in selecting the structures and places to house their operations and employees in New York City. Some of those media companies attempt to make a public statement about their presence and dominance through spatial consideration

LIKE OYSTERS OBSERVING THE SUN THROUGH THE WATER

Created by ANDREA AVILA *NOVEMBER 28TH, 2012*

DESCRIPTION

Tasting an oyster is like tasting the sea. Throughout the history of New York's lucrative oyster trade, a metaphor for the waterfront seems to gradually form: a metaphor wherein the hard designation of an edge is cast off. A relationship between land and water emerges in such a way as to disintegrate the definitive boundaries once separating the two. The oyster itself seems to be a metaphor for an edgeless seasons, the way in which it allows itself an object, accreting a fluid substance that supports its shell. Anatomically it is metaphorical too — one shell is flat while the other is curved, the concept shell having the sole ability to attach itself to objects.

Waterfront metaphors emerge in the various points of data: the sites where water sites purposefully into Manhattan's rigid grid, the oyster houses that embody the

NEW YORK ON THE BROADWAY STAGE

Created by ROBIN LICHTENSTEIN *NOVEMBER 28TH, 2012*

PROJECT INFO   **DATA**   **ARGUMENTS**

Hard Knock Life

(Interpreting New York Through Song)

by Robin Lichtenstein, at Dec. 11, 2012, 11:38 p.m.

Song Name: Hard Knock Life

Song Link:

confronted with the challenge of mapping nonlinear events via an interactive timeline; the challenge of handling fuzzy dates via a data model that wanted specific days and times; and the challenge of mapping their own work schedules onto those of our software developers. And over the years, as students' stories accumulated on the map, we discovered points of intersection between those stories. Those intersections often allowed for temporal entanglements to reveal themselves—for the "deep time" of the media city to emerge.

Although all of these maps are illuminating and innovative in their own ways, some would have to be adapted to allow for the mapping of *media* places, networks, events. Some are built on databases nicely designed to support the methodologies and epistemologies of humanities and social scientific research, but they often leave some to be desired in terms of aesthetics. Some, conversely, are rather tightly controlled gems of interaction and graphic design that, unfortunately, either wouldn't scale or allow for easy replication, or that wouldn't easily accommodate the messiness of a deep map, with its lack of authorial control and incorporation of myriad voices and media formats. Of course we've examined mostly print-based and digital projects—but that's only because it's hard to experience a soundwalk, or handle material cartographic objects, via a *book*. It's important to remember that our maps can take any format that suits our methods and subjects and audiences. We can draw bits of insight from each of these projects and piece together our own deep mapping strategies and platforms that fit the particularities of our own urban media interests.

These examples demonstrate the value of mapping as a method and of thinking of the map itself as a medium to which we have to apply our critical faculties. Infrastructure, in its material and spatial dimensions, lends itself particularly well to mapping. And when we add a historical dimension to the study of media infrastructure, the deep map is particularly well suited to illuminating the complex materialities—political economic, technological, social, biological—and entangled temporalities of infrastructure. A deep map of the media city can help to reveal that urban mediation—even the "sentient city"—emerged well before Gibson's Singapore or even Benjamin's Paris; its origins are instead rooted in deep time—a time we can inhabit on a deep map.

Acknowledgments

I'd like to thank Seija Ridell and Jani Vuolteenaho, organizers of the "Spectacular/Ordinary/Contested Media City" conference at the Helsinki Collegium for Advanced Studies in May 2014; the conference afforded me the opportunity to share an early version of this text as a keynote. Rebecca Ross provided much valuable feedback and encouragement, and an anonymous reviewer of this manuscript helped me to fine-tune many arguments. I also owe a great debt of gratitude to Josie Holzman, who assisted with the collection of all the images you see here, and to Rory Solomon, Jane Pirone, and Jessica Irish, with whom I thought about and tinkered with maps over the past several years.

Thanks, too, to colleagues who've discussed with me the preliminary ideas that have taken shape here, and who've allowed me to reprint or adapt portions of previous publications for use in this text.

Shannon Mattern is associate professor in the School of Media Studies at the New School in New York. She is author of *The New Downtown Library* (Minnesota, 2007).

Made in the USA
Middletown, DE
08 May 2017